D1272433

SOUTH DAKOTA

Past and Present

Christine Petersen

rosen publishing's
**rosen
central®**

New York

For Jule, my favorite South Dakotan

Published in 2011 by The Rosen Publishing Group, Inc.
29 East 21st Street, New York, NY 10010

Copyright © 2011 by The Rosen Publishing Group, Inc.

First Edition

All rights reserved. No part of this book may be reproduced in any form without permission in writing from the publisher, except by a reviewer.

Library of Congress Cataloging-in-Publication Data

Petersen, Christine.
South Dakota: past and present / Christine Petersen. — 1st ed.
    p. cm. — (The United States: past and present)
Includes bibliographical references and index.
ISBN 978-1-4358-9496-9 (library binding)
ISBN 978-1-4358-9523-2 (pbk.)
ISBN 978-1-4358-9557-7 (6-pack)
1. South Dakota—Juvenile literature. I. Title.
F651.3.P47 2010
978.3—dc22

                                                                    2010002584

Manufactured in Malaysia

CPSIA Compliance Information: Batch #S10YA: For further information, contact Rosen Publishing, New York, New York, at 1-800-237-9932.

On the cover: Top left: Meriwether Lewis and William Clark leading an expedition. Top right: Buffalo grazing on the prairie grass of South Dakota. Bottom: Mount Rushmore.

Contents

Introduction   **5**

Chapter 1
The Geography of South Dakota   **7**

Chapter 2
The History of South Dakota   **14**

Chapter 3
The Government of South Dakota   **20**

Chapter 4
The Economy of South Dakota   **27**

Chapter 5
**People from South Dakota:
Past and Present**   **32**

Timeline   **38**

South Dakota at a Glance   **39**

Glossary   **41**

For More Information   **42**

For Further Reading   **44**

Bibliography   **45**

Index   **47**

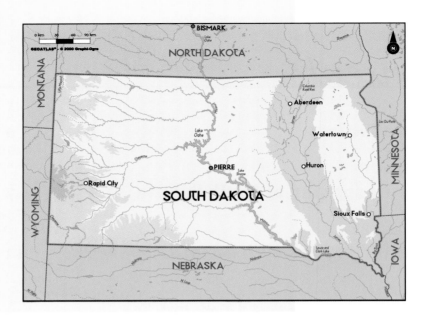

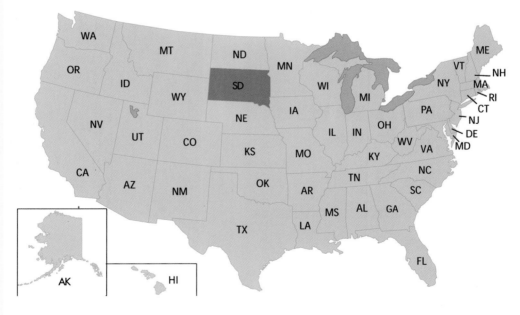

South Dakota became the fortieth U.S. state in 1889. It lies at the heart of the Great Plains, a region known for lush grasslands and rich soil.

Introduction

In the spring of 1832, a small steamboat called *Yellow Stone* pulled away from the docks in St. Louis, Missouri. Traveling west and then north on the Missouri River, the *Yellow Stone* soon crossed into an untamed part of North America. Its goal was to reach distant fur trading posts 2,000 miles (3,218 kilometers) upriver. Artist George Catlin was one of the *Yellow Stone*'s few passengers. He took the steamer to the end of the line, then spent months floating downriver on a canoe. Catlin stopped often to paint and visit Native American villages along the route.

George Catlin's paintings gave many nineteenth-century Americans their first look at the frontier landscape and its people. The letters he sent back to a New York newspaper were as detailed as his paintings. While passing through present-day South Dakota, he wrote, "The surface of the country is gracefully and slightly undulating, like the swells of the retiring ocean after a heavy storm. And everywhere covered with a beautiful green turf, and with occasional patches and clusters of trees. The soil in this region is also rich, and capable of making one of the most beautiful and productive countries in the world."

Catlin's prediction was correct. Thanks to its fertile soil, South Dakota has become one of the most important agricultural regions in the United States. But much more than farms can be found in the state of South Dakota. From prairies to mountains, its natural environment is breathtaking and diverse. The state's fascinating human history reaches back more than eleven thousand years, to the last ice age. Yet South Dakota is also a thoroughly modern place, home to industries, arts, and science. Its people represent a blend of the past and present—American Indians and descendants of European settlers, along with African American, Asian American, and Hispanic residents who moved there more recently. Visitors can explore the many natural and man-made treasures that South Dakota has to offer. Come and explore!

Chapter 1

THE GEOGRAPHY OF SOUTH DAKOTA

South Dakota's boundaries were decided in 1889, when it became the fortieth state in the United States. But the land is far more ancient. Its first rock layers formed as a result of volcanic activity on Earth's surface more than three billion years ago. During later eruptions, magma became trapped below and between these layers. This liquid rock slowly hardened to form granite. At the same time, hot magma caused older rocks to bend and partially melt. A new type of rock called quartzite resulted. Granite and quartzite are exceptionally durable rocks and form the base of South Dakota's landscape.

Changes in sea level left these rocks underwater several times in the past five hundred million years. Earth's ancient oceans swarmed with algae and shelled animals similar to snails and squid. When they died, their bodies drifted to the seafloor. Calcium carbonate, a chemical released from the decaying shells, formed layers of limestone atop the older rocks.

To see any of these rocks, visit the Black Hills, a mountain range in the southwestern corner of the state. The Black Hills formed about sixty million years ago when two tectonic plates, or pieces of Earth's surface, collided and buckled upward.

The highest point in the Black Hills—and in South Dakota—is Harney Peak. Carved from the same ancient granite as this peak are

In 1948, Korczak Ziolkowski began carving the massive Crazy Horse Memorial in the Black Hills. The sculpture honors the Lakota warrior who fought to protect his people's land and way of life in the 1800s.

two of the world's largest man-made sculptures, Mount Rushmore and the Crazy Horse Memorial. Approximately two hundred natural sculptures can be found inside the Black Hills. These caves were formed by the slow trickle of water through limestone. The Jewel Cave and Wind Cave are among the longest in the world, each with passages measuring more than 130 miles (209 km).

Beginning two million years ago, Earth's climate entered an exceptionally cool period of glaciation. Thick sheets of ice formed and melted time after time. These dragged across the landscape, tearing up rocks and soil along their path. The last glaciers reached eastern South Dakota approximately thirty thousand years ago. Their tremendous weight pressed down on the land, making it flatter and lower than regions to the west.

On the Prairie

South Dakota lies at the heart of a widespread grassland, in a region known as the Great Plains. Grasslands are found in many parts of the world, but those in the Great Plains are called prairie. The prairie is lush with grasses and wildflowers. These plants die off in winter and grow anew each spring.

Trees may be found alongside prairie streams and lakes but are scarce on the open plains. This is because prairie is prone to drought. South Dakota averages only 14 to 25 inches (36 to 63 centimeters) of precipitation per year, depending on the region.

Unlike most trees, prairie plants are adapted to survive drought. Their complex root systems reach far to gather water from the soil. For example, while the stem of western wheatgrass may be only 2 feet (.6 meters) tall, its roots extend twice as deep.

With drought comes fire. Prairie fires clear out young trees and shrubs, which grow back slowly. Grasses also burn but quickly recover. Native Americans knew this and used fire to attract bison, which fed on young plant sprouts.

South Dakota's tallgrass prairie requires wet soil and occurs only in the east, where annual average precipitation is higher. Native tallgrasses such as big bluestem and switchgrass may be 7 feet (2 meters) tall. Wildflowers such as milkweed, blazing star, and pasque flower grow among the grasses. They attract a bounty of pollinators, from bees and beetles to butterflies and hummingbirds. Mixed-grass prairie is found across the rest of the state. These plants grow smaller, and some, such as prickly pear, hold water in their leaves to resist drought.

Creatures Great and Small

If you could hop in a time machine and travel back one hundred million years, South Dakota would look very different. Rivers wandered across a wide, swampy plain, flowing toward a shallow inland sea at the center of the continent. This period in Earth's history is called the Cretaceous period.

Many reptiles thrived in the Cretaceous period, but the most impressive were dinosaurs. Massive beasts such as *Edmontonia* and *Triceratops* grazed on land plants. Despite this simple lifestyle, their appearance was fearsome. Covered in thick, bony plates and spikes, they could have been mistaken for dragons. Such defenses were crucial to survive the attacks of *Tyrannosaurus rex*. Measuring 40 feet (12 m) from nose to tail and bearing a mouthful of daggerlike teeth, *T. rex* lived up to its name, which means "tyrant king."

Sixty-five million years ago, the reign of reptiles came to an end when a dramatic change in climate caused the extinction of many animals on Earth. But one small group of dinosaurs survived the Cretaceous extinctions. Like *T. rex*, they belonged to a group called therapods. All therapods could maintain a warm body (rather than needing to absorb heat from the sun). These creatures had new features to aid their success: feathers and wings. Today, this group of therapod dinosaurs lives all around us. They are more commonly called birds.

Grab your binoculars—more than four hundred bird species can be found in South Dakota! One of the best places to see them is the Coteau des Prairies. This large table of land is located on the drift prairie in eastern South Dakota. Dotted with wetlands, it attracts millions of ducks, geese, and other waterfowl. Some birds stop to rest during their long migration; others stay to nest. Songbirds nest and migrate through the river corridors and prairies, where plants, insects, and seeds provide food in abundance.

Prairie dogs are a symbol of this landscape. Their large underground communities once spread across much of western South Dakota. For decades these rodents were hunted as pests. Scientists now realize that up to 130 other species live in and around prairie dog towns. These include black-footed ferrets, coyotes, and hawks. Laws now limit hunting, and visitors can see blacktail prairie dogs at sites such as Custer State Park in the Black Hills.

Prairie dogs live in large groups, excavating complex underground passages. These rodents were long thought of as pests, but people now recognize their important role in the prairie environment.

According to the South Dakota Department of Game, Fish, and Parks, tallgrass and mixed-grass prairie historically covered 95 percent of the state. Over the past 150 years, most of this has been converted to farms. Rich soil in the tallgrass region supports the state's most productive cropland. Remaining prairie exists in pockets that have been protected by the government and private organizations or landowners.

A Changing Landscape

East of the Missouri River, South Dakota's geography is distinguished by gently rolling hills that hide lush wetlands and hundreds of lakes.

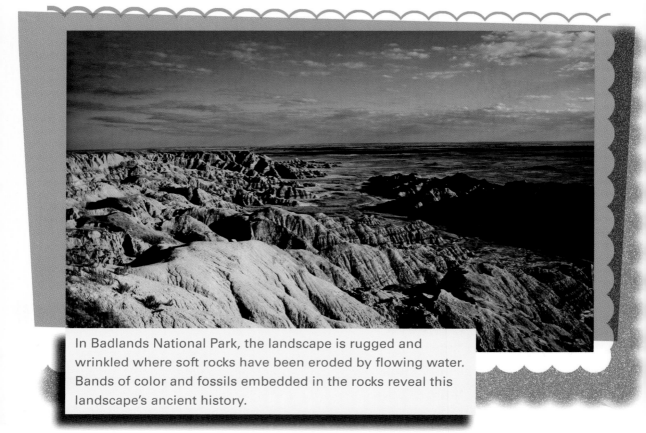

In Badlands National Park, the landscape is rugged and wrinkled where soft rocks have been eroded by flowing water. Bands of color and fossils embedded in the rocks reveal this landscape's ancient history.

Within these hills are deep layers of broken rock called drift, which were deposited by the movement of ancient ice. Lakes formed wherever isolated blocks of ice melted in place. The James River marks the main path along which glacial meltwater drained southward.

West of the river, soils are drier and the landscape more dramatic. Steep-sided buttes rise from the plains, and tree-lined creeks cut snaking canyons into the earth. The White River Badlands provide an impressive example of this process of erosion. Rocks here were formed in ancient seas and riverbeds. Over the past five hundred thousand years, the river has cut through these soft rocks, revealing colorful layers and creating strange patterns.

The Black Hills are unlike any other part of the state. They're home to plants and animals usually found in high mountains. Bighorn sheep and yellow-bellied marmots perch on the rocky slopes and live among ponderosa pine, aspen, and white spruce trees.

Fossils found in this part of the state provide a glimpse of life during the last ice age. Glaciers never reached the western half of South Dakota; instead, this region looked like Alaska's tundra. Woolly mammoths, giant beavers, and other large mammals dominated the land. They were ideally suited for the harsh ice age environment, with thick fur and stores of fat. Many of these species went extinct about eleven thousand years ago. Scientists long believed that large ice age mammals were unable to survive a warmer climate. Recent evidence suggests they may have been hunted to extinction by a species that arrived in North America during the ice age: humans.

Chapter 2

THE HISTORY OF SOUTH DAKOTA

Eleven thousand years ago, South Dakota's climate began to warm after a long ice age. Ice sheets and glaciers were replaced by a lush landscape of woodland and prairie. Early human hunters, called Paleo-Indians, found this land ideal. Two mammoth fossils found in the White River Badlands reveal that Paleo-Indians hunted with sharp stone spear points and designed bone tools to cut and carve meat. As these large mammals became extinct, Indian hunters sought out new prey, especially bison.

Over the centuries, Plains Indian cultures became quite complex. Large villages grew up alongside the Missouri and other rivers. The people gardened and made pottery and began to trade with distant tribes. Hunting became even more efficient with the invention of weapons such as the bow and arrow.

The Arikara, Cheyenne, Crow, and Pawnee were among many tribes on the northern plains in the seventeenth century. Their lives would change when European fur traders arrived in Minnesota. Traders offered guns and other goods to the Chippewa Indians in exchange for animal furs. This new firepower gave the Chippewa an advantage in battle over other Minnesota Indians, whom they called Nadouessioux—"enemies." Europeans shortened the name to Sioux.

Before European settlement, Sioux tribes spread across the Great Plains. When South Dakota became a state in 1889, the remaining Sioux were moved to reservations like this one along the Cheyenne River.

The Sioux were not one tribe but several, separated by language. While moving west to avoid Chippewa raids, bands of Dakota- and Nakota-speaking Sioux settled east of the Missouri River. The largest group, called the Lakota, continued west. By 1762, they had reached the Black Hills. The Sioux gradually forced the Arikara and other small tribes north. They became excellent horsemen and hunters, following bison across the prairie. For the Lakota in particular, the Black Hills became sacred land.

Settlers dug prairie sod to provide insulation for their houses. "Bricks" containing soil and dense prairie grass roots slowed down the rushing, bitter winter winds and kept the houses cool in summer.

Settling the Plains

In the 1740s, two French brothers, François and Louis-Joseph de La Vérendrye, became the first Europeans to explore the Great Plains. But white men remained a rare sight in South Dakota until 1817, when fur trader Joseph La Framboise established a trading post, later known as Fort Pierre. Conflict erupted in the 1830s as settlers began to establish farms and ranches on Indian hunting grounds. The U.S. government and tribal leaders attempted to solve the problem by establishing an official Sioux territory.

The Homestead Act of 1862 offered settlers 160 acres (64 hectares) of free land outside the Sioux territory. Free land was tempting, but there was a catch. Settlers had to "prove up" by building a home and raising crops within five years, or the government would take back the land. It was a huge challenge to prove up in the Dakotas. The prairie offered few trees to use as building material. Settlers earned the nickname of "sodbusters" because they learned to use blocks of grass and soil as bricks. Drought, blizzards, tornadoes, and swarms of insects killed their crops. Many sodbusters gave up in misery or died before proving up.

Yet the population continued to grow. In 1860, the U.S. Census Bureau recorded a non-Indian population of approximately five thousand in South Dakota. Just thirty years later, that number had increased to almost 350,000. One factor was the discovery of gold in the Black Hills in 1874. Railroad lines also improved travel into the Dakotas.

In 1889, many people celebrated the acceptance of South Dakota as the fortieth state. Meanwhile, U.S. troops began to move American Indians onto reservations scattered across the state. The Great Sioux Agreement of 1889 had opened much of their former territory to

The Big Muddy

In 1682, French explorer René-Robert Cavelier, Sieur de la Salle, sailed down the Mississippi River from Illinois to the Gulf of Mexico. A vast amount of western land drained into the river. La Salle claimed this territory for France, calling it Louisiana. President Thomas Jefferson purchased Louisiana from French emperor Napoleon Bonaparte in 1803. The Louisiana Purchase increased the area of the United States by 828,800 square miles (2,146,582 square km). It also offered new routes for trade and land for settlement. Jefferson sent Meriwether Lewis and William Clark on an expedition up the Missouri River and west to the Pacific Ocean. In 1804, they passed through South Dakota. Between late August and mid-October, the expedition camped at approximately thirty-five sites around and near the Missouri River. They met various Indian tribes and recorded many new plants and animals, including vast herds of bison. After two years, Lewis and Clark returned to Washington, D.C., reporting that the West was a wide-open land full of wildlife and other resources that would be useful to American settlers.

American author and humorist Mark Twain once said that the Missouri River is "too thick to drink and too thin to plow." Residents call it the Big Muddy because of its brown color. But they depend on this river and treasure its role in their natural environment. The modern Missouri is a very different river than Lewis and Clark knew. Heavy flooding in the 1940s led to extensive crop damage along the river's banks. Congress authorized construction of four major dam systems along the river to control flooding and provide irrigation water to nearby farms. These dams are also designed as hydroelectric power stations that provide electricity to South Dakota and the surrounding Great Plains states.

white settlement. The free-roaming, hunting people of the Great Plains were now required to live on small reservation farms.

Staying Strong

The twentieth century posed a new set of challenges for South Dakotans. The United States participated in two world wars before the century was even half over. Between these wars, in the 1930s, the entire Great Plains region suffered a severe drought. The prairie soil had already been over-

Record flooding on the Missouri River in April 1952 carried water through downtown Pierre, South Dakota. Soon after, the U.S. government approved the construction of dams on the river to control future floods.

farmed. High temperatures and a lack of rain over a period of years caused crops to fail. Loose, exposed soil began to blow away, producing choking dust storms known as the Dust Bowl. This period overlapped with the Great Depression, during which the national economy failed and many Americans were out of work. Severe flooding on the Missouri River in 1993 caused crop failures once again, and on June 24, 2003, the state experienced an outbreak of sixty-seven tornados. South Dakota and its people have flourished in the face of these difficulties.

Chapter 3

THE GOVERNMENT OF SOUTH DAKOTA

The nineteenth century was a time of constant change in American history. Among the most significant events of the time was the settlement of territories west of the Mississippi River. When a territory's population of white citizens reached sixty thousand, the process of application for statehood could begin. Delegates were elected to represent the population at a convention, where a constitution was written. If the U.S. Congress approved this document and the goals it represented, a new state was admitted to the Union.

Why choose statehood? Citizens had no voice in a territorial government. Governors were appointed, rather than elected. There was no way to vote the governor out, and he or she had total control over lawmaking—for better or worse. But a state would have laws and elections: through the democratic system, citizens might create change.

After achieving statehood, South Dakotans elected Arthur C. Mellette as their first governor and, after some dispute, chose the small town of Pierre as their capital city. The state constitution of South Dakota was written to "establish justice, insure tranquility, provide for the common defense, promote general welfare, and preserve to ourselves and to our posterity the blessings of liberty." This document has continued to grow and change over the years.

Arthur C. Mellette encouraged President Benjamin Harrison to grant statehood to South Dakota. He helped write the new state's constitution and was elected its first governor in 1889.

At the Capitol

State governments are modeled after the federal system, with three branches: legislative, executive, and judicial. The South Dakota Legislature makes new laws and passes the annual state budget. This legislature is bicameral, or consists of two parts—a senate and a house of representatives. Thirty-five legislators are elected to the senate, while the house has seventy members. One senator and two representatives are chosen from each of South Dakota's thirty-five election districts. They serve a two-year term and may be reelected for a maximum of four consecutive terms. Each year, the house and senate drafts, reviews, and may pass hundreds of bills. Because the legislative session lasts only thirty-five to forty days, its work must be efficient. The governor may call additional sessions when necessary.

The governor leads South Dakota's executive branch. Every bill passed by the legislative branch must receive his or her signature, although in most cases the governor has the option to veto them. Governors also command the state armed forces and appoint cabinet members—those officials who run departments that keep the state running. The cabinet oversees transportation, schools and public lands, the treasury, and more. A lieutenant governor, attorney general, and secretary of state are other cabinet members who work closely with the governor. All members of South Dakota's executive branch are elected to four-year terms and may serve only two consecutive terms. They may run for reelection at a later date, however.

South Dakota's laws are upheld by its judicial system, which consists of three levels of courts. At the local level, trials are heard by municipal court judges. Their primary responsibility is to rule on

South Dakota's state capitol building is located in Pierre. Completed in 1910, its design is similar to that of the U.S. Capitol Building, with a domed entry and a wing on each side.

minor criminal cases and legal disputes between citizens. Circuit courts are located in seven parts of the state. Thirty-eight judges are elected to handle more serious cases in these courts. The governor appoints five justices to sit on the state supreme court, but their terms must be approved by a popular vote after three years. Supreme court justices mostly review appeals—cases that have already passed through the lower courts but are still in dispute.

South Dakotans also elect members to participate in the U.S. Congress. Two senators represent each of the fifty states, but population determines the number of representatives a state sends to the U.S. Congress. South Dakota has one member. U.S. senators serve six-year terms, while representatives must run for reelection after two years.

Local and Tribal Governments

The state constitution of 1889 established that South Dakota would be divided into counties. It also allowed groups of people to establish townships. Both counties and townships were authorized to establish rules of local government, as long as these followed the laws passed by South Dakota's legislature. Today, South Dakota has sixty-six counties. Each is governed by a board of commissioners who are elected by residents of the county. More than three hundred townships exist in South Dakota. In 2009, their populations ranged widely. Ada, northeast of the Black Hills, had just 26 citizens, while Sioux Falls was home to more than 154,000. Whatever its size, a township is governed by an elected mayor and council.

South Dakota is also home to nine reservations, each of which has an independent government. Sioux tribes use a system equivalent to

PAST AND PRESENT

Law and Order

In the late 1800s, South Dakota lay at the heart of the Wild West. Towns such as Deadwood grew up quickly in the Black Hills gold rush country. They attracted more than miners. Merchants came to provide equipment and food. Bankers were ready to cash in gold, while innkeepers provided food and lodging. To others, gold country offered the possibility of making a fortune the easy way—by gambling. James Butler "Wild Bill" Hickok is among the most famous of the gamblers who lived in Deadwood. Also an excellent sharpshooter, he was rumored to have killed thirty-six men in the West. Deadwood was filled with such characters—including some women, such as Martha "Calamity" Jane Canary. These gunslingers had moments of kindness, taking care of those in their community. But they lived by their own laws.

The new state of South Dakota quickly overcame its reputation for lawlessness. In part, this was achieved by recognizing that citizens play an important role in government.

In 1898, South Dakota's constitution was amended to allow the processes of initiative and referendum. An initiative is a law proposed by citizens. At least 5 percent of state voters must sign a petition in support of the proposed initiative. Then it goes onto the ballot and will become law if a majority of voters approve. When legislation is passed by the state congress, the governor may still veto it. But the governor must honor legislation that has passed by initiative. Citizens may propose a referendum when legislators pass a law that does not have popular support. Democracy works because it has checks and balances—ways of ensuring that no level of government gains too much power. Referendums allow South Dakotans to overturn laws that seem inappropriate to their way of life.

the U.S. federal government, with leadership at the band, tribal, and national levels. Delegates are elected from each reservation. Each tribe elects representatives to sit on a council, led by a chairperson who is elected by the council members. The council's job includes managing the tribal budget, passing laws, and appointing judges. It also negotiates with local, state, and federal governments to protect tribal lands and rights. The reservations are also divided into districts, each of which has a local council. At every level of tribal government, councilors must make decisions about education, health and social services, and other issues that affect the people.

Chapter 4

THE ECONOMY OF SOUTH DAKOTA

South Dakota has traditionally been an agricultural state, and that remains true today. Slightly more than half of its population lives in rural areas where agriculture is the most important industry. Farms and ranches take up 90 percent of the state's land area. About half of South Dakota farms are smaller than 500 acres (202 ha). Many of these farms are family-run, passed down from parents to children.

In 2008, South Dakota ranked among the top U.S. exporters of soybeans, wheat, sunflowers, and grains used to feed livestock. Corn is another important crop. These crops are grown on the rich soils of the eastern drift plains. Ranches and feedlots, most located west of the Missouri River, produce cattle and hogs. South Dakota is also an important producer of dairy products. Although a large percentage of these agricultural products remain in the United States, some are exported to foreign nations. South Dakota's trade partners include Canada and Mexico, as well as countries in Europe and Asia.

Working Away from the Farm

Many of the agricultural products raised in the state require processing before being exported. Employees of the state's manufacturing industry do this work. They clean, sort, and package food for

Agriculture is the most important industry in South Dakota. Many eastern farms are dotted with prairie potholes. Formed by melting glaciers about eleven thousand years ago, these potholes catch rainwater.

shipping, taking steps to ensure that food does not spoil during transport.

Tourism provides many jobs west of the Missouri River. Each year, millions of visitors come to the Black Hills, Badlands, and other state and national parks. In 2008, they spent more than $2.4 billion. This was an increase over previous years, despite a national recession when unemployment was high and people were generally spending less. It's a reminder that beautiful places are valuable at any time.

Although gold supplies have decreased, South Dakota has large supplies of other useful minerals. Limestone and quartzite are mined primarily in the Black Hills. Sand and gravel are found around the state, providing materials for road construction and building. Timber is another natural resource that supports the state economy. South Dakota attempts to protect the state's small natural forests while harvesting valuable amounts of pine, oak, and other tree species.

Tourism is another vital industry in the state. Many visitors are drawn to Mount Rushmore National Memorial, which depicts the faces of U.S. presidents George Washington, Thomas Jefferson, Theodore Roosevelt, and Abraham Lincoln.

South Dakota has only a few cities. Sioux Falls, Rapid City, and Aberdeen are the largest. But these cities have thriving populations that play an important role in the state economy. Sioux Falls is home to the University of South Dakota. Many hospitals are located there as well. The city supports numerous financial institutions and other businesses. Retail sales and restaurants provide another boost to the city-based economy. South Dakotans who work in these jobs, as well as teachers, government employees, and various professionals, are part of the state's service industry.

Over the past few decades, South Dakota has welcomed new companies involved in electronics and computer manufacturing. Farm

Tatanka Wakan

For the Sioux and other Indians on the plains, bison were more than a source of food. They were the center of an entire way of life. Family groups moved seasonally to follow the huge herds. Hunters might kill large numbers of bison at one time. The meat was preserved for winter, and the rest of the body was used in practical ways. Blankets, clothing, and moccasins were made from bison fur. Some skins were scraped clean to make rawhide, which was used for tepee covers, drum covers, and much more. Bison bones were carved to form tools or cups, spoons, and other household utensils. Sioux relied on, and respected, the bison so much that they called it *Tatanka Wakan*, meaning "sacred bison." By some estimates, the United States was home to sixty million bison in the mid-1800s. But the population declined quickly after European settlement on the plains. White hunters sought the valuable furs, and the U.S. government ordered bison killed to keep Indians under control. By the 1890s, only a few hundred wild bison survived in the entire nation.

A small herd of American bison was eventually restored to South Dakota's Black Hills. Today, approximately 1,500 bison graze the mixed-grass prairie of Custer State Park in the Black Hills, making it a popular tourist attraction. The bison represent more than one-tenth of North America's entire bison population. Larger numbers of bison can be found on ranches. Bison meat is considered a heart-healthy alternative to beef. Some ranchers also use bison as a way to restore ranchland that has been damaged by years of overgrazing by cattle. Bison move frequently while feeding, rather than feeding until the grass is gone. This allows prairie grasses to thrive, and it attracts native species to follow the bison. Bison ranching connects South Dakota's modern economy to the environment and cultures of its past.

machinery and construction equipment are also built there. Each year brings new ideas and industries. One example is the construction of a massive science laboratory at the former Homestake Mine in the Black Hills. For more than 125 years, Homestake was South Dakota's most productive gold mine. Physicists will use its deep tunnels to study dark matter, a type of particle that has not yet been observed but is believed to fill much of the "empty" space in the universe. Although South Dakota remains deeply connected to its agricultural roots, its people continue to move toward a bright and innovative future.

In 2009, South Dakota's governor, Mike Rounds (*right*), and businessman T. Denny Sanford met 4,850 feet (1,478 m) underground to fete the opening of the Sanford Underground Science and Engineering Laboratory.

Chapter 5

PEOPLE FROM SOUTH DAKOTA:
PAST AND PRESENT

South Dakota has always had a small population compared to other U.S. states. Nonetheless, it has been home to many remarkable people—from American Indian leaders to sports legends.

Respected Leaders

Gertrude Simmons Bonnin (1876–1938) was born on the small Yankton Sioux Reservation, located along South Dakota's southeastern border with Nebraska. By this time, reservation life had already begun to create poverty, disease, and alcoholism among many Sioux. Young Bonnin was fortunate. A scholarship allowed her to study music in Boston. In 1900, she published several essays using her Sioux name, Zitkala-Sa ("Red Bird"). Her opera, called "Sun Dance," was the first written by an American Indian. But Bonnin's real concern was American Indian rights. She worked to protect remaining Indian lands and encourage tribal leadership on reservations.

Tom Daschle (1947–) was born in Aberdeen, South Dakota. The first person in his family to graduate from

Gertrude Simmons Bonnin was also known by her Sioux name, Zitkala-Sa ("Red Bird"). She became famous as a writer and opera composer, but she spent much of her life working for American Indian rights.

South Dakotans chose George McGovern to represent them in Congress. In 1972, he ran unsuccessfully as the Democratic candidate for president.

college, he was elected to two terms in the U.S. Congress before running for Senate. Daschle rose to become the leader among Senate Democrats, the first South Dakotan chosen for that honor. He left office in 2005 and spends his time writing, teaching, and speaking.

Hubert Humphrey Jr. (1911–1978) was raised in Wallace, South Dakota. After college, he moved to Minnesota and was elected to three terms as that state's U.S. senator. He became vice president in the administration of President Lyndon B. Johnson (1965–1969) and was widely admired for his support of social issues such as civil rights. Humphrey failed to win the 1968 presidential election, but Minnesotans soon reelected him to the Senate. He remained in office until his death.

George McGovern (1922–) began his political career as one of South Dakota's representatives to the U.S. House. He later became a U.S. senator, and in 1972 ran unsuccessfully

Fighting for the Land

The Fort Laramie Treaty of 1868 promised that "no white person or persons shall be permitted to settle upon or occupy any portion of" Sioux territory. The Sioux expected to live on this sacred land in western South Dakota forever. But that agreement lasted only six years. Miners began to flood into the Black Hills after the discovery of gold in 1874. Rather than enforcing the treaty, the U.S. government tried to buy the land. When local Lakota leaders refused, the government ordered them to move away. Sitting Bull (1831–1890), a Lakota chief and holy man, called thousands of warriors together. They easily won the first battle against troops led by General George Armstrong Custer. But the U.S. soldiers kept coming. Many Lakota people died, and the survivors were sent to reservations. Sitting Bull eventually surrendered. In 1890, this fearless warrior was shot during a riot at South Dakota's Standing Rock Reservation.

Russell Means (1939–) was born on the Pine Ridge Reservation. As a young man, he joined the American Indian Movement (AIM), an organization that worked for civil rights. In 1973, Means and other AIM activists led a siege of a small Pine Ridge town called Wounded Knee. This had been the site of a terrible massacre of Lakota people by U.S. soldiers in 1890. AIM activists held off FBI agents and police for seventy-one days, demanding better conditions on reservations and the return of the Black Hills to the Sioux. The U.S. Supreme Court eventually reviewed the case and agreed. It awarded $122 million in payment. The tribes have not accepted the payment because it is the land they value. Russell Means is now an actor, writer, and artist. He also works with the Pine Ridge Reservation and the United Nations, seeking improved living conditions for American Indians and native people worldwide.

for president. McGovern remains active as a professor and a supporter of programs to prevent world hunger.

Authors, Artists, and Athletes

George Lee "Sparky" Anderson (1934–) South Dakota has also produced many fine athletes. Sparky Anderson was admitted to the Baseball Hall of Fame in 2000. His career as a Major League Baseball player and manager began in 1955 and included three World Series wins.

Tom Brokaw is a native South Dakotan who became one of the most respected journalists on television. He is also the author of several best-selling books.

Tom Brokaw (1940–) has been on national television for more than forty years. Born in Webster, South Dakota, he studied political science at the University of South Dakota. After graduating in the 1960s, he was hired by NBC News and went on to become one of America's most respected broadcast journalists. Brokaw is also a best-selling author and has made documentaries on some of the most newsworthy topics of our time, including civil rights, immigration, AIDS, and climate change.

Oscar Howe (1915–1983) was born on the Crow Creek Indian Reservation. As a small child, he began to draw pictures illustrating the stories told by his elders. After serving in World War II, Howe studied art and was soon in demand for his murals, paintings, and sculptures. He spent most of his career at the University of South Dakota as a professor and museum director. Oscar Howe's work represents Plains Indian art but is also unique and modern.

William Mervin Mills (1938–) Among the most inspirational stories is that of Billy Mills. Mills was born into poverty on the Pine Ridge Indian Reservation. As a twelve-year-old boy, he took up sports to find leadership and positive influences after his parents died. Long-distance running became his passion. At the University of Kansas, Mills earned three All-American titles from the National Collegiate Athletic Association (NCAA). He later qualified for the 1964 Olympic Games in Tokyo. Mills's performance in the 10,000-meter (6.2-mile) run had viewers on the edge of their seats. He broke out of third place just before the finish line, becoming the first American to win the gold in that event. In 1983, his story was made into a feature film called *Running Brave*. Today, Mills is an inspirational speaker who works with American Indian youth.

Timeline

11500 BCE	The earliest hunting tribes settle on land now known as South Dakota.
1600s	Sioux tribes move westward from Minnesota onto the Great Plains.
1743	French explorers François and Louis-Joseph de La Vérendrye become the first white people to visit the northern plains.
1803	President Thomas Jefferson purchases Louisiana from France, doubling the size of the United States.
1804–1906	The Lewis and Clark Expedition explores the Missouri River through South Dakota, continuing west to the Pacific Ocean.
1862	The Homestead Act encourages settlers to farm and ranch on the Dakota plains.
1868	The Fort Laramie Treaty designates land as a Great Sioux Reservation, supposedly inaccessible to white settlement. This territory includes much of western South Dakota and the Black Hills.
1874	The U.S. government allows miners to seek gold in the Great Sioux Reservation.
1876	Sitting Bull and his warriors defeat General Custer at the Battle of Little Bighorn.
1889	South Dakota is accepted as the fortieth U.S. state. The Great Sioux Agreement opens Sioux land to settlement and moves the Indians onto separate reservations.
1898	South Dakota becomes the first state to allow initiatives and referendums when proposing new legislation.
1930s	South Dakota and other Great Plains states experience a drought that creates the Dust Bowl; an economic depression strikes the United States.
1993	Flooding on the Missouri River causes extensive crop damage.
2008	Construction begins on a major underground science laboratory at Homestake Mine, a former gold mine in the Black Hills.

South Dakota at a Glance

State motto:	"Under God the People Rule"
State capital:	Pierre
State flower:	Pasque flower
State bird:	Chinese ring-necked pheasant
State tree:	Black Hills spruce
Statehood date and number:	1889; North and South Dakota were admitted simultaneously, becoming the thirty-ninth and fortieth states
State nickname:	Mount Rushmore State
Total area and U.S. rank:	75,800 square miles (196,321 square km); sixteenth largest state
Population:	804,000
Length of coastline:	0 miles
Highest elevation:	7,242 feet (2,207 m), at Harney Peak
Lowest evelation:	962 feet (293 m), at Big Stone Lake

State flag

State seal

Major rivers:	Missouri River, James River, Cheyenne River
Major lakes:	Lake Oahe, Lake Francis Case, Lewis and Clark Lake
Hottest recorded temperature:	120 degrees Fahrenheit (48 degrees Celsius), July 3, 1936
Coldest recorded temperature:	-58°F (-50°C), February 17, 1936
Origin of state name:	Named for the Dakota Indian tribe
Chief agricultural products:	Corn, cattle, soybeans, wheat, hogs
Major industries:	Agriculture, tourism, computer parts and electronics manufacturing, ethanol fuel production, food processing, gold mining, financial services

Chinese ring-necked pheasant

Pasque flower

GLOSSARY

appeals Disputed legal cases that are taken to higher courts.

bicameral A legislature divided into two separate bodies, a house and senate.

climate The long-term pattern of temperature and precipitation in a region.

drift Layers of rock rubble left by glaciers.

drought A period of little rain.

economy The production and consumption of goods that result in jobs and spending.

erosion The movement of weathered soil and rocks by water and wind.

export To send to another country for sale or exchange.

extinct Having no remaining members of a species.

glaciation A period when the climate is especially cold and icy.

initiative A law proposed by citizens.

magma Liquid rock that is produced from deep inside Earth.

particle A very small piece of something.

pollinator An animal or insect that moves pollen between plants, aiding their reproduction.

prairie A grassland habitat in North America.

rawhide An animal skin that has been scraped clean of fur.

recession A period when economic trade declines and unemployment may be high.

referendum A vote to test citizens' support of a law.

tectonic plates A large segment of Earth's surface that moves slowly over time.

territory An area of land chosen by or set aside for a certain group.

therapods A group of warm-blooded dinosaurs that gave rise to birds.

treaty An agreement between governments.

FOR MORE INFORMATION

Homestake Mining Company

160 West Main Street

Lead, SD 57754

(605) 584-3110

Web site: http://www.homestaketour.com

Discover the amazing history of gold mining in the Black Hills through this site. It is one of the oldest and most productive mining companies in the region.

Jewel Cave National Monument

11149 U.S. Highway, Building B12

Custer, SD 57730

(605) 673-8300

Web site: http://www.nps.gov/jeca/index.htm

On this site, you can obtain directions to this cave—one of the longest in the world—or learn about the cave's amazing geology and the creatures that call it home.

The Mammoth Site

1800 Highway 18 Truck Route

P.O. Box 692

Hot Springs, SD 57747

(605) 745-6017

Web site: http://www.mammothsite.com

Learn why dozens of ice age mammoths were trapped in this small location in the Black Hills and how paleontologists are uncovering the fossils.

Mitchell Prehistoric Indian Village

3200 Indian Village Road

Mitchell, SD 57301

(605) 996-5473

Web site: http://www.mitchellindianvillage.org/index.php

Archaeologists are learning a great deal about the lives of early Native Americans by studying artifacts at this thousand-year-old village. Search the site to see pictures and read what their research has revealed.

South Dakota Museum of Geology

501 E. St. Joseph Street

Rapid City, SD 57701

(605) 394-2467

Web site: http://museum.sdsmt.edu/exhibits

If you can't go to the Black Hills, try a virtual tour of the Museum of Geology. You'll see fascinating rocks and fossils found in South Dakota and around the world.

South Dakota State Historical Society

900 Governors Drive

Pierre, SD 57501

(605) 773-3458

Web site: http://history.sd.gov

This site contains many original historical records, summaries of state history, and links to online museum exhibits.

Web Sites

Due to the changing nature of Internet links, Rosen Publishing has developed an online list of Web sites related to the subject of this book. This site is updated regularly. Please use this link to access the list:

http://www.rosenlinks.com/uspp/sdpp

FOR FURTHER READING

Bright, Michael. *Geological and Fossil Evidence* (Timeline: Life on Earth). Chicago, IL: Heinemann Library, 2009.

George, Charles. *The Sioux* (The North American Indians). San Diego, CA: Thomson Gale, 2004.

Hobbs, Will. *Go Big or Go Home*. New York, NY: HarperCollins, 2009.

Horner, Jack. *Digging Up Dinosaurs*. Helena, MT: Farcountry Press, 2007.

Jay, Michael. *Ice Age Beasts* (Prehistoric Animals). Chicago, IL: Heinemann-Raintree, 2004.

Lynch, Wayne. *Prairie Grasslands* (Our Wild World Ecosystems). Minnetonka, MN: NorthWord, 2006.

McDaniel, Melissa. *South Dakota* (Celebrate the States). New York, NY: Marshall Cavendish Benchmark, 2007.

McNeely, Marian Hurd. *The Jumping-Off Place*. Pierre, SD: South Dakota State Historical Society, 2008.

Patent, Dorothy Hinshaw. *The Buffalo and the Indians: A Shared Destiny*. New York, NY: Clarion Books, 2006.

Reilly, Edward J. *Sitting Bull: A Biography*. Westport, CT: Greenwood Press, 2007.

Sheinkin, Steve. *Which Way to the Wild West?* New York, NY: Roaring Brook Press, 2009.

St. Antoine, Sara, ed. *Stories from Where We Live: The Great American Prairie*. Minneapolis, MN: Milkweed Editions, 2001.

Steele, Christy. *Pioneer Life in the American West* (America's Westward Expansion). Milwaukee, WI: World Almanac Library, 2005.

Woodward, John. *The Secret World of Prairie Dogs*. Chicago, IL: Heinemann-Raintree, 2004.

BIBLIOGRAPHY

Catlin, George. *Letters and Notes on the Manners, Customs, and Condition of the North American Indians* (Vol. I). Minneapolis, MN: Ross and Haines, Inc., 1965.

Center for American Progress. "Senator Tom Daschle." Retrieved November 21, 2009 (http://www.americanprogress.org/experts/DaschleSenatorTom.html).

Davis, Leslie. *Hunters of the Recent Past*. New York, NY: Routledge, 1989.

Day, John. "About Oscar Howe." Oscar Howe Memorial Association, 1996. Retrieved November 2, 2009 (http://www.oscarhowe.org).

Dingus, Lowell, and Timothy Rowe. *The Mistaken Extinction: Dinosaur Evolution and the Origin of Birds*. New York, NY: W. H. Freeman and Company, 1998.

Gries, John Paul. *Roadside Geology of South Dakota*. Missoula, MT: Mountain Press Publishing Company, 1996.

Harmon, Greg. "June Tornadoes in South Dakota Tie National Record." NOAA National Weather Service Forecast Office, October 27, 2005. Retrieved November 9, 2005 (http://www.crh.noaa.gov/fsd/storms/tor062403/sdtor062403.php).

Hogan, Edward P. *The Geography of South Dakota*. Sioux Falls, SD: The Center for Western Studies, 1998.

IUCN Red List of Threatened Species. "Bison Bison (American Bison)." Retrieved November 2, 2009 (http://www.iucnredlist.org/apps/redlist/details/2815/0/full).

Jackson, Donald. "The Short, Dramatic Life of the Steamboat *Yellow Stone*." *American Heritage*, May/June 1987, Volume 87/Number 4.

Jones, Susan. "Becoming a Pest: Prairie Dog Ecology and the Human Economy in the Euroamerican West." *Environmental History*, October 1999.

Lyndon Baines Johnson Library and Museum. "Vice President Hubert Horatio Humphrey." Retrieved November 21, 2009 (http://www.lbjlib.utexas.edu/johnson/archives.hom/FAQs/humphrey/HHH_home.asp).

Mattoon, Rick. "Assessing the Midwest Floods of 2008 (and 1993)." Federal Reserve Bank of Chicago, July 10, 2008. Retrieved November 9, 2009 (http://midwest.chicagofedblogs.org/archives/2008/07/mattoon_flood_b.html).

McGovern Center for Leadership and Public Service. "George McGovern." 2009. Retrieved November 21, 2009 (http://www.mcgoverncenter.com/george.htm).

Milton, John R. *South Dakota: A History*. New York, NY: W. W. Norton & Company, 1977.

MSNBC.com. "Tom Brokaw." 2009. Retrieved November 21, 2009 (http://www.msnbc.msn.com/id/4364148).

O'Brien, Sharon. *American Indian Tribal Governments*. Norman, OK: University of Oklahoma Press, 1993.

Raventon, Edward. *Island in the Plains: A Black Hills Natural History*. Boulder, CO: Johnson Books, 1994.

Running Strong for American Indian Youth. "Who Is Billy Mills?" 2009. Retrieved October 29, 2009 (http://www.indianyouth.org/billymills.html).

South Dakota Department of Game, Fish, and Parks. "Bird Watching Guide for South Dakota State Parks and Recreation Areas." Retrieved September 15, 2009 (http://www.sdgfp.info/Publications).

South Dakota Department of Game, Fish, and Parks. "Prairie Offers Habitats." Dakota Wild, December 2006. Retrieved October 15, 2009 (http://www.sdgfp.info/wildlife/Education/Projwild/DakotaWildDec06Final.pdf).

South Dakota Geological Survey. "South Dakota Geology." October 29, 2009. Retrieved November 7, 2009 (http://www.sdgs.usd.edu/geologyofsd/geosd.html).

South Dakota Legislature. "South Dakota Constitution." 2009. Retrieved October 30, 2009 (http://legis.state.sd.us/statutes/Constitution.aspx).

South Dakota Science and Technology Authority. "Sanford Underground Laboratory at Homestake." 2009. Retrieved November 28, 2009 (http://www.sanfordunderground laboratoryathomestake.org).

South Dakota State Historical Society. "Chronology of South Dakota History." Retrieved April 22, 2009 (http://www.sdhistory.org/soc/soc_hist.htm).

South Dakota State Historical Society. "Reaching Out to the Past." April 30, 2009. Retrieved September 27, 2009 (http://www.sdsmt.edu/wwwsarc/past.html).

State of South Dakota. "The South Dakota Legislature" January 2009. Retrieved November 2, 2009 (http://legis.state.sd.us/sessions/2009/guide.pdf).

U.S. Census Bureau. "South Dakota QuickFacts." November 17, 2009. Retrieved November 23, 2009 (http://quickfacts.census.gov/qfd/states/46000.html).

USDA Economic Research Service. "South Dakota Fact Sheet." October 21, 2009. Retrieved October 31, 2009 (http://www.ers.usda.gov/statefacts/SD.HTM).

USGS, Northern Prairie Wildlife Research Center. "Ecoregions of North Dakota and South Dakota." August 3, 2006. Retrieved August 27, 2009 (http://www.npwrc.usgs.gov/resource/habitat/ndsdeco/sodak.htm).

WETA Washington. "New Perspectives on the West—People from A to Z Index." 2001. Retrieved September 23, 2009 (http://www.pbs.org/weta/thewest/people/a_c/index.htm).

Zitkala-Sa. *Dreams and Thunder: Stories, Poems, and the Sun Dance Opera*. Lincoln, NE: University of Nebraska Press, 2005.

A

American Indian Movement (AIM), 35
Anderson, "Sparky," 36

B

Badlands, 12, 14, 28
bison, 9, 14, 15, 18, 30
Black Hills, 7–8, 11, 13, 15, 17, 24, 25, 28,
    30, 31, 35
Bonaparte, Napoleon, 18
Bonnin, Gertrude Simmons, 32
Brokaw, Tom, 36

C

Canary, "Calamity" Jane, 25
Catlin, George, 5
Clark, William, 18
Crazy Horse Memorial, 8
Custer, George Armstrong, 35

D

Daschle, Tom, 32, 34
Deadwood, 25
Dust Bowl, 19

F

Fort Laramie Treaty of 1868, 35
fur trade, 5, 14, 17, 30

G

gold, discovery of, 17, 25, 35
Great Depression, 19
Great Sioux Agreement of 1889, 17

H

Hickok, "Wild Bill," 25
Homestead Act of 1862, 17

Howe, Oscar, 37
Humphrey Jr., Hubert, 34

J

Jefferson, Thomas, 18
Johnson, Lyndon B., 34

L

La Framboise, Joseph, 17
La Salle, René-Robert Cavelier, 18
Lewis, Meriwether, 18
Louisiana Purchase, 18

M

McGovern, George, 34, 36
Means, Russell, 35
Mellette, Arthur C., 20
Mills, William Mervin, 37
Missouri River, 5, 11, 14, 15, 18, 19, 27, 28
Mount Rushmore, 8

N

Native Americans, 5, 6, 9, 14–15, 17, 19,
    24, 26, 30, 32, 35, 37

P

Pierre, 17, 20
prairie dogs, 11

S

Sitting Bull, 35
sodbusters, 17
South Dakota
    economy of, 5–6, 11, 27–31
    geography of, 5, 6, 7–13

government of, 20–26, 34
history of, 5, 6, 7, 10, 14–19, 30
people from, 32–37
South Dakota Department of Game, Fish,
    and Parks, 11

U

University of South Dakota, 29, 36, 37

V

Vérendrye brothers, 17

T

Twain, Mark, 18

Y

Yellow Stone, 5

About the Author

Christine Petersen is the author of more than three dozen nonfiction books for children and young adults. A former science teacher and naturalist who lives in Minnesota, she was pleased to learn more about the geography and history of her neighboring state of South Dakota. Petersen is a member of the Society of Children's Book Writers and Illustrators.

Photo Credits

Cover (top left), p. 1 (top left) David David Gallery/Getty Images; cover (top right), p. 1 (top right) © www.istockphoto.com/Jim Parkin; cover (bottom) Mark Harris/Getty Images; pp. 3, 7, 14, 20, 27, 32, 38 Bloomberg via Getty Images; p. 4 (top) © GeoAtlas; p. 8 © www.istockphoto.com/Magdalena Marczewska; p. 11 © www.istockphoto.com/ Andy Gehrig; pp. 12, 40 (right) © www.istockphoto.com; pp. 15, 33 © The Granger Collection; p. 16 © North Wind/North Wind Picture Archives; p. 19 Francis Miller/ Time-Life Pictures/Getty Images; p. 21 State Historical Society of North Dakota D0217; p. 23 Matthew McVay/Getty Images; p. 28 Frank Oberle/Getty Images; pp. 29, 31 © AP Images; p. 34 Bill Eppridge/Time-Life Pictures/Getty Images; p. 36 Alex Wong/Getty Images; p. 39 (left) Courtesy of Robesus; p. 40 (left) © Tom Vezo/Peter Arnold.

Designer: Les Kanturek; Editor: Bethany Bryan;
Photo Researcher: Marty Levick